SHAKESPEARE
AUTHORSHIP

SHAKESPEARE AUTHORSHIP
A SUMMARY OF EVIDENCE

By
GILBERT STANDEN

CECIL PALMER
FORTY-NINE
CHANDOS
STREET
W.C.2

FIRST
EDITION
1930
COPY-
RIGHT

PR
2947
.O9
S8

Made and Printed in Great Britain at the KEMP HALL PRESS, LIMITED,
in the City of Oxford

SHAKESPEARE AUTHORSHIP

It happens to us all at times to consider what are the foundations for the faith that is in us, and to take stock of our beliefs, and of our reasons for holding them. In early life we either conform to the views of our instructors, or at any rate it becomes necessary or politic to appear to do so. Inevitably, to most of us, there comes a period when we must question the authority in charge of the moulding of our minds and ideas, and frequently we find it to be personal and arbitrary in its opinions. In nothing can this be more clearly demonstrated than in historical matters as presented to our youthful and immature judgment. There is a modern tendency to override conventions and preconceived ideas, and to find much to be said on the part of diametrically opposite theories. Sentimentality is out of date, with its attitude of awe-struck reverence. We find, and are glad to recognize, that great men of the past need no longer be beatified and spoken of with bated breath. They were indeed great, but their human side, their weaknesses, their failings, and above all their sense of humour, have hitherto been in great part ignored. Now it is just this human side, when duly considered, that makes them real and attractive ; it brings them out of shadowland into daylight, and in place of an insincere veneration gives us a warm and personal interest.

SHAKESPEARE'S PERSONALITY

On a quite insufficient basis a structure of fiction has been built up around the imaginary personality of England's greatest poet. It is hardly to be believed that the reverential worshippers at his shrine have more than scant knowledge of the very few facts that are undoubtedly true and beyond question regarding their idol, and even if the few traditions be added to these facts, there is still a very insubstantial basis for the suppo-

SHAKESPEARE AUTHORSHIP

sition that the author of the plays and poems was the actor whose life began and ended in complete obscurity, while its interim period is almost entirely a matter of conjecture.

In his work, "Shakespeare Personally," David Masson says: "Shakespeare's life, in respect of external circumstances, divides itself into three parts or stages:

(1) 1564–1586 (?) : *ætat.* 22 (?). *Stratford-on-Avon.*

(2) 1586 (?)–1604 (?) : *ætat.* 22 (?)-40 (?). *London.*

(3) 1604 (?)–1616 : *ætat.* 40 (?)-52. *Stratford-on-Avon again.*

This, with some uncertainty as to the particular years that are queried, is the authentic map, summary, or ground-plan of Shakespeare's life, as it emerges from the records. It is a very simple and natural English life—a life of three stages. But what a superstructure, what a filling up!"

Quite so, and here at once is an instance of flights of ingenious imagination providing a substitute for an inconvenient absence of matter and evidence. Imagination is necessary to an author, but invention is not admissible in serious history or biography, and from such a setting it should be rigidly excluded.

THE FACTS OF HIS LIFE

Such facts as are actually known to be true have been drawn up by Mr. William Poel, founder and director of the Elizabethan Stage Society, and consist of the following:

1564. Baptism, April 26th. "Gulielmus fillius Johannes Shakspere."

1582. Marriage. "William Shagspere and Anne Hathwey," November 28th.

1583. Daughter's baptism, May 26th. "Susanna daughter to William Shakspere."

1585. Twin's baptism, Feb. 2nd. "Hamnet & Judith sonne & daughter to William Shakspere."

1594. Named as one of the actors, paid March 15th, for shewing before the Queen at Christmas "twoe severall comedies or enterludes."

SHAKESPEARE AUTHORSHIP

1596. Assessed 13s. 4d. on property valued at £5 in the parish of St. Helens; he was now lodging in Bankside.

1596. Son dies; buried August 11th. First application to Heralds' College for coat of arms.

1597. Buys New Place and an acre of land for £60.

1598. Acts in Ben Jonson's comedy, "Every Man in his Humour."

1598. Called Gentleman and Householder in town documents of Stratford. Richard Quiney wants to borrow £30 from him. Coat of arms granted by Heralds' College. Mother's claim to the arms of Arden of Park Hall refused, 1599. Father dies intestate; buried Sept. 8th, 1601.

1599. Globe Playhouse built. The two Burbages held five shares; Shakspere, Heminge, Phillips, Pope, and Kempe, five shares between them.

1602. Buys 107 acres of land near Stratford for £320. Also a cottage and quarter acre of land at the back of New Place.

1603. Second on list of players receiving scarlet cloth as King's Servants. Acts in Ben Jonson's "Sejanus."

1605. Buys for £440 half the unexpired lease of Stratford tithes. Lodging now or recently with Mountjoy, a wig-maker, in Silver Street, Cripplegate. Receives 30s. from a fellow player, Phillips, for a memorial ring.

1607. His brother, Edmund, a player, buried at St. Saviour's, Southwark, the great bell being tolled, Dec. 31st.

1608. Godfather to William Walker, son of Henry Walker, mercer and alderman. Takes one-seventh share in Blackfriars Theatre. His share in Globe Theatre reduced to one-twelfth, and ultimately to one-fourteenth.

1609. Wins case against John Addenbroke, for payment of £6 and £1 5s. costs, who then absconded, and Shakspere sues Thomas Horneby, who had gone bail for debtor.

1610. Buys 20 acres from John Combe.

SHAKESPEARE AUTHORSHIP

1612. Signs affidavit in the *Bellot v. Mountjoy* case. Described as of Stratford-on-Avon, Gentleman, of the age of 48 or thereabouts. (Signature is " Wilm Shaxpr.")

1613. Buys house in Blackfriars for £140.

1614. A legatee in John Combe's will. Secures from John Combe's heir, William, a deed of indemnity against personal loss if Common-fields are enclosed. Does not support protest against the enclosure.

1614. " My cosen, Shakspere, comyng yesterday to towne, I went to see him how he did."—T. Greene, Nov. 17th.

1616. Receives first draft of his will, Jan. 25th, Revises and signs will, March 25th. Assets : £350 in cash, personal belongings, and estate bought for £1,200. The mayor and leading townsmen sign as witnesses. Buried in chancel of Parish Church. Entry in register : Burials, 1616, " April 25 Will Shakspere gent."

SHAKESPEARE AUTHORSHIP

TRADITIONS

1634. That he satirized his friend, John Combe, in an epitaph "fastened" to his monument. *Norwich Diary*.

1649. That King Charles read his plays more often than the Bible. *James Cooke*.

1650. That he held wit combats with Ben Jonson. *Fuller's Worthies*.

1656. That his father was "a merry-cheeked" old man. *Archdeacon Plume*.

1662. That he drank too hard at a merry meeting with Drayton and Jonson, and died of a fever; and that in his last years at Stratford he lived at the rate of a thousand a year. *John Ward, Vicar of Stratford*.

1663. That he instructed Taylor in the part of Hamlet, and that the impersonation was imitated by Betterton. *Downes*.

1672. That he said he had to kill Mercutio in the third Act of "Romeo and Juliet" to save his play. *John Dryden*.

SHAKESPEARE AUTHORSHIP

1677. That "Troilus and Cressida" was maimed by the omission of Act and Scene divisions, and that this was the fault of the actors. *John Dryden.*

1680. That his father was a butcher, that he was once a schoolmaster, that he returned home once a year, and that Sir William D'Avenant seemed contented enough to be thought his son. *Aubrey.*

1688. That he poached Sir Thomas Lucy's deer. *William Fulman.*

1693. That he was apprenticed to a butcher, that he began as a play-house servitor, and that his wife and daughter wished to be buried in his grave. *Dowdall.*

1698. That in the writing of his plays he was guilty of immorality. *Jeremy Collier.*

1700. That he played Adam in "As You Like It." *Oldys.*

1708. That he died a Papist. *Rev. Richard Davies.*

1709. That his father was a wool-dealer, that he went to Stratford free school, that he received £1,000 from Southampton, that he got Ben Jonson's first play acted, that he played the Ghost in "Hamlet," that the Queen wished him to write a play to show Falstaff in love, that Susanna was his favourite daughter, and that his last years were spent in ease, retirement, and the conversation of his friends. *Rowe*.

1710. That he received an autograph letter from King James. *Lintot*.

1726. That he wrote for gain and not for glory. *Pope*.

1750. That he held horses for theatre goers. Old tradition quoted by *Colley Cibber*.

1760. That he planted a mulberry tree at New Place. *R. B. Whelen*.

1762. That he engaged in a drunken bout at Bideford. *British Magazine*.

THE SHAKESPEARE CULT

There does not, on the face of it, appear to be any particular reason to connect the subject of the above meagre biographic

SHAKESPEARE AUTHORSHIP

record with the versatile author of those plays and poems whose stupendous knowledge and insight into human life and nature is an enduring source of delight and wonder to the world. Shakespeare worship is a part of national emotionalism, it has become almost as vital a matter as religion, and any student who seeks to make an intelligent inquiry into the history and career of the man who has been generally accepted as the author lays himself open to be treated as a heretic, or even as an atheist. A learned and witty French professor recently expressed surprise at the omission of a Saint Shakespeare from the calendar. To such an extent has the absurdity grown of a superstructure built up by the devices of uncontrolled fantasy !

The Shakespeare cult arose in the eighteenth century under the impetus given by David Garrick, and continued into the romantic period of the nineteenth, and even to the first decade of the twentieth century. The first reaction against this uncritical enthusiasm occurred in 1909, when Frank Harris published his book, "The Man Shakespeare and His Tragic Life Story." He says: "I want to liberate Englishmen so far as I can from the tyranny of Shakespeare's greatness . . . . he is like the Old-Man-of-the-Sea on the shoulders of our youth, he has become an obsession to the critic, a weapon to the pedant, a nuisance to the man of genius."

THE GROUP THEORY

During the last eighty years various theories have been advanced as to the authorship of the Shakespeare literature. In 1848 J. C. Hart published a book in New York, entitled "The Romance of Yachting." The following remarkable sentence occurs in this work: "Who were the able literary men who wrote the dramas imputed to Shakespeare?" In 1857 Delia Bacon published "The Philosophy of Shakespeare's Plays Unfolded." Nathaniel Hawthorne wrote a sympathetic preface to this book, in which the theory of a secret Shakespeare society, under the leadership of Sir Walter Raleigh, was suggested. Other

SHAKESPEARE AUTHORSHIP

members of this society were Francis Bacon, the Earl of Oxford, Lord Paget, and Lord Buckhurst. Various writers since that date have suggested theories about the authorship, among the claimants put forward being Francis Bacon, the 3rd Earl of Southampton, the 5th Earl of Rutland, the 6th Earl of Derby and the 17th Earl of Oxford. The recent discoveries of the Shakespeare Fellowship have provided justification for all these theories. It has been found from the Exchequer documents in the Public Record Office that the average expenditure on the Army and Navy from 1586 to 1604—that is during the whole period of the Anglo-Spanish War—amounted to no less than 72 per cent. of the national income. Another discovery, also derived from Elizabethan Exchequer documents, shows that the Earl of Oxford was in receipt of a salary of £1,000 a year from the Secret Service Fund during the whole of this period. All the great historical patriotic plays, such as Marlowe's " Edward II " Shakespeare's " King John," and " Henry V," were produced during this period. The inevitable inference would seem to be that a Propaganda Department was established by the Government in order to inculcate and encourage patriotism and loyalty to the reigning dynasty during the war years.

The evidence for all this, together with full references to the documents in the Public Record Office, showing the expenditure on Secret Service and on the Army and Navy during the Anglo-Spanish War, will be found in two articles by Captain B. M. Ward, published in English in the Review "Anglo-Americaine" in April 1929 and April 1930. It is interesting to find that this latest discovery confirms the opinions expressed by J. C. Hart and Delia Bacon in 1848 and 1857 as to the origin of the Shakespeare literature. It also explains what Mr. Harold Bayley has shown so convincingly in "The Shakespeare Symphony," published by him in 1906. In this book he shows "that the Elizabethan Dramatists constitute an Orchestra playing a great Symphony."

It is this same unity of aim and purpose, accomplished by means of a national organi-

SHAKESPEARE AUTHORSHIP

zation receiving its original impulse from the Queen herself, which accounts for the fact that Professor Connes in his " Shakespeare Mystery," published in 1927, has been able to argue so plausible a case in favour of all the Shakespeare candidates put forward by him. The fact is they were all members of the group, and all concerned in one way or another with the production of the plays. This applies even to William Shakspere of Stratford, who most certainly was one of the group, and actually went so far as to claim the premier position, as we know from Ben Jonson's epigram :

> " Poor poet-ape, who would be thought our chief."

THE MASTER MIND

Although our researches prove that a group of authors was responsible for the Shakespeare literature, it is equally incontrovertible that one member of this group stands out as a great poet. The late President of the Shakespeare Fellowship, Sir

SHAKESPEARE AUTHORSHIP

George Greenwood, hit the nail on the head when he described the First Folio of 1623 as the work of " many pens and one Master Mind." The Master Mind cannot have been William Shakspere of Stratford, because the mere possession of genius cannot account for the fact that the plays and poems were written by a person of high culture, of exceptional erudition, and above all, of aristocratic origin and surroundings. The doctrine of inspired genius fails to account for the above conditions. Genius is evident, but only a man of the highest education, of the widest experience of foreign travel, and of Courts, both at home and abroad, could by any reasonable likelihood have written of all these matters from an intimate personal knowledge, making use in his writings of the most extensive vocabulary ever possessed by any author. The words used in Shakespeare are estimated by Max Müller in his " Science of Languages," 1885, to amount to 15,000—twice as many as are used by any other writer—an explanation of the " several hands " employed in the plays.

SHAKESPEARE AUTHORSHIP

There is no record of William Shakspere having been one of the actors in Lord Leicester's company which their patron took with him to the Low Countries when he went there as the Queen's representative in 1585, yet it has been alleged that it was in some such manner the actor obtained his knowledge of men and matters foreign to his native soil. The answer to this surmise is that the travelling experiences of English theatrical companies were necessarily confined to Protestant countries, and that Italy was never visited by them, while it is manifest that the author of the plays and poems was intimately acquainted with Courts and cities in both of those Catholic countries, Italy and France.

THE CASE FOR OXFORD

If it appears incredible that William Shakspere of Stratford can have possessed the undoubted culture and attainments to qualify him as the Master Mind, there is no other more likely candidate for that position than

SHAKESPEARE AUTHORSHIP

the 17th Earl of Oxford. The following seven quotations, when considered in combination, constitute the case for supposing him to be the real author.

(1) In 1578, when William Shakspere of Stratford was fourteen years old, Gabriel Harvey, in an address of welcome to the Earl of Oxford, writes, strongly urging him to give up literature, and to devote himself to a life of action. The following is a translation of some of the Latin verses in which Gabriel Harvey composed his address of welcome:

" For a long time past Phœbus Apollo has cultivated thy mind in the arts; British poetical measures have been sung by thee long enough.

. . . . .

" O thou hero worthy of renown, throw away the insignificant pen, throw away bloodless books, and writings that serve no useful purpose. Now must the sword be brought into play, now is the time for thee to sharpen the spear."

SHAKESPEARE AUTHORSHIP

At this period Oxford was twenty-eight years old, and less than 250 lines of verse had at that time been published in his own name. Very few more had been published in his own name at the time of his death in 1604.

(2) In 1586, when William Shakspere was twenty-two, and was still living at Stratford, "A Discourse of English Poetrie" by William Webbe was published. In this treatise occurs the following sentence:

"I may not omit the deserved commendations of many honourable and noble Lords, and Gentlemen, in Her Majesty' Court, which in the rare devices of poetry, have been and yet are most skilful, among whom the Right Honourable Earl of Oxford may challenge to himself the title of the most excellent among the rest."

(3) In 1589 Lord Lumley in his "Arte of English Poesie" mentions:

"a crew of courtly makers (poets) Noblemen and Gentlemen, who have written excellently well, as it would appear if their doings could be found out and made public with the rest, of which number is first that noble gentleman Edward Earl of Oxford."

(4) The following is another extract from Lord Lumley's "Arte of English Poesie" published in 1589:

"For such doings of theirs as I have seen do deserve the highest price: the Earl of Oxford and Master Edwards for comedy and interlude."

(5) Francis Meres, in 1598 (by which time a number of "Shakespeare" plays had been published) placed Oxford's name first in the list of those "best for comedy."

(6) Arthur Collins, in 1772, wrote of Oxford as:

"an excellent poet and comedian (whose) compositions ... are lost or worn out."

(7) Sir Sidney Lee ("Dictionary of National Biography") writes:

"No specimens of his dramatic productions survive."

SHAKESPEARE AUTHORSHIP

The first of these quotations shows Oxford to have been a well-known poet and prolific writer in 1578. At this time, and indeed for that matter even up to the time of his death in 1604, hardly more than 250 lines of verse had been openly acknowledged by him as their author. He must therefore have been publishing anonymously from a very early period—none but his earliest efforts having been issued in his own name. We may conclude that he is a poet of whose verses only a few early specimens have survived. The second and third quotations show him to have been the leader of a group of anonymous courtier poets.

The fourth and fifth quotations show him to have been regarded later on as one of the best dramatists of the period.

The sixth and seventh quotations show that none of his dramas have survived.

For two reasons it was not possible for Oxford to claim his position publicly:

(1.) He was employed on Government Secret Service, and the fact that he inspired and subsidized patriotic plays had to be kept secret.

(2). As a nobleman, it was quite contrary to the social conventions of the time that his name should appear as the author of plays written for the public stage.

The claims for Lord Oxford as the Master Mind of the group have been set forth in the following books:

" 'Shakespeare' Identified." By J. T. Looney, 1920.

" Shakespeare through Oxford Glasses." By Captain H. H. Holland, 1923.

" Shakespeare Sonnets and Edward de Vere." By Dr. G. H. Rendall, 1930.

" The Case for Edward de Vere as Shakespeare." By Percy Allen, 1930.

In 1928 Captain Ward published an exhaustive biography of the 17th Earl of Oxford, which is a mine of information as to the life and activities of this nobleman.

Not a single manuscript or writing of any sort has come down to us from the hand

SHAKESPEARE AUTHORSHIP

of William Shakspere of Stratford, with the exception of half-a-dozen doubtful and execrably written signatures.

Oxford has left between thirty and forty letters in the British Museum, and in Lord Salisbury's collection at Hatfield House, all written in a clear, legible hand, the "sweet Roman hand" of "Twelfth Night." If anything, the letters improve in legibility, rather than otherwise, as Oxford grew older, a fact which seems to suggest that at the close of his life he was accustomed to write for the press, and had to consider the question of making every letter clear and unmistakable in the eyes of an unintelligent compositor.

SHAKESPEARE A PSEUDONYM

The name William Shakespeare seems to have been used from the outset as the pseudonym of the leader of the group from 1593, when it was first employed under the Dedication of "Venus and Adonis" to the 3rd Earl of Southampton. The name would seem to have been chosen partly on account of its similarity to the name of the actor, William Shakspere, who replaced Marlowe in the group immediately after his murder in 1593, and partly because the Director of War Propaganda could be fittingly described as a spear shaker. This is clearly shown in the case of the following Quartos, where the name on the Title Page is divided by means of a hyphen, thus: Shake-speare.

"Richard II," Editions of 1598, 1608, and 1615.

"Richard III," Editions of 1598, 1605, and 1612.

"Henry IV," Editions of 1599, 1604, 1608, 1613, and 1622.

"Hamlet," Edition of 1603.

"The Sonnets," Edition of 1609.

"King Lear," Editions of 1608 and 1619.

This seems to be an evident indication that the name was a pseudonym, and was intended to suggest something connected with war. Thomas Fuller (1608-1661) whose "Worthies of England" was published the year after his death, writes under the heading of "Worthies of Warwickshire":

SHAKESPEARE AUTHORSHIP

" William Shakespeare was born at Stratford-on-Avon in this county, in whom three eminent poets may seem in some sort to be compounded. 1. *Martial*, in the warlike sound of his surname (whence some may conjecture him of a military extraction) *Hasti-vibrans*, or Shake-speare. 2. *Ovid*, the most natural and witty of all poets. . . . . 3. *Plautus*, who was an exact comedian, yet never any scholar, as our Shakspeare (if alive) would confess himself."

While Fuller does not seem to have had any inkling of the existence of a War Propaganda Department, he evidently saw some connection between the name Shakespeare and military affairs.

Although the name would seem to have been originally intended to represent the head of the Department, as well as his representative the actor from Stratford-on-Avon, no doubt it also came to include later on all the members of the group.

SHAKESPEARE AUTHORSHIP

FRANCIS BACON

The name of Francis Bacon has been mentioned in connection with the Shakespeare literature for a longer period than that of any other member of the Department, with the sole exception of William Shakspere of Stratford. There seems to be very little doubt that, from the first, Bacon, who may well have been one of the " grand possessors " mentioned in the preface to " Troilus and Cressida," acted as editor of the group, a function which he probably continued to perform after Oxford's death in 1604. If this is the case, it is to Bacon that we owe the preservation of the seventeen plays which had never been printed before the Folio of 1623, and he is in all likelihood the author of " The Tempest," which he appears to have written as an allegorical introduction to the whole volume. But peace with Spain occurred in 1604, just after Oxford's death, and the reason for a national War Propaganda Department no longer existed. Although there was no excuse for the official continuance

SHAKESPEARE AUTHORSHIP

of a national Department of State subsidized from Secret Service funds, it is quite clear that Bacon realized the importance of preserving the literature that had been produced during the period of the long Anglo-Spanish War.

Miss Lilian Winstanley, Lecturer in English in the University College of Wales, has shown in her books, " Hamlet and the Scottish Succession," 1921, and " King Lear," 1923, that these plays were produced for the immediate purpose of defeating the machinations of the Catholic League, and to assure the Union of the Crowns and religious freedom in the person of James I. She thus proves that political propaganda was not confined to the Historical plays, and that it was continued under the Stuart dynasty. It is not unlikely that Francis Bacon was in charge of the Group of the old War Propaganda Department after the death of Oxford, and the peace with Spain, both of which events occurred in 1604, the year of the accession of James I.

SHAKESPEARE AUTHORSHIP

CIRCUMSTANTIAL EVIDENCE

That Oxford was not only the head of the Department, as we know from the fact of his salary of £1,000 a year, but was also the chief writer and poet of the group, may be argued either from the literary side or from the point of view of external evidence.

Here the case for Oxford as Shakespeare is considered from the point of view of the circumstances under which *Shake-speares Sonnets* were first published in 1609, making use of the discoveries in Parish Registers made by Colonel B. R. Ward, and put forward by him seven years ago in "The Mystery of Mr. W.H.," published by Cecil Palmer.

The case is one of circumstantial evidence, and I cannot do better at this point than quote the remarks of the Lord Chief Justice, Lord Hewart, in his direction to the Jury in a recent murder trial:[1] " You have been told twice," remarked he, " and I will remind you for the third time, that this is a case of circumstantial evidence. One never quite

[1] That of William Podmore, in March, 1930.

knows what meaning those words convey to somebody else's mind. Circumstantial evidence is sometimes spoken of in language of apology, as if it were some minor or less-compelling kind of evidence. Is that so? Circumstantial evidence, that is to say, the evidence of accumulative surrounding circumstances all pointing in one direction, circumstantial evidence is contrasted with direct evidence, that is to say the evidence of an eye-witness. But one cannot forget that an eye-witness may sometimes be mistaken; there may be the interference of grudge or spite. Circumstantial evidence is free from those blemishes.

Circumstantial evidence consists in this: that when you look at all the surrounding circumstances you find such a series of undesigned, unexpected coincidences that, as a reasonable person, you find your judgment is compelled to one conclusion. If the circumstantial evidence is such as to fall short of that standard, if it does not satisfy that test, if it leaves gaps, then it is of no use at all. Now, nobody in this case professes to have seen any blows struck upon Mr. Messiter. What is said is that when you bring an impartial mind to bear upon all the available material, you are driven to the conclusion that this act was done by one man, and one man alone."

AUTHORSHIP OF THE SONNETS

The problem before us is the authorship of the Sonnets published in Quarto as " Shake-speares/Sonnets/Neuer before Imprinted/At London/By G. Eld for T.T. and are/to be solde by William Aspley./1609."

The following facts may be taken as admitted by all scholars:

(1) The volume was printed without the author's permission.

(2) The initials T. T. stand for a publisher, Thomas Thorpe.

William Shakspere of Stratford-on-Avon is generally credited with the authorship, but for the following reasons this ascription is improbable:

(*a*) The dedication of the volume, initialed

SHAKESPEARE AUTHORSHIP

by T. T., refers to the author as " our ever-living poet." This phrase assumes that the person alluded to is no longer living, and William Shakspere did not die till 1616.

(*b*) Although several of these sonnets can be interpreted in a manner seriously compromising the character of the author, no explanation or protest was ever made by him.

(3) Sonnet No. CXI opens in the following manner:

> O, for my sake do you with fortune chide,
> The guilty goddess of my harmful deeds,
> That did not better for my life provide
> Than public means which public manners breeds.
> Thence comes it that my name receives a brand,
> And almost thence my nature is subdued
> To what it works in, like the dyer's hand.

Now William Shakspere of Stratford was a professional actor, and would not be likely to run down his profession in this way.

Many other reasons might be adduced

SHAKESPEARE AUTHORSHIP

against the common ascription to the Stratford man, such as the obvious fact that these poems show over and over again the tastes and habits of thought of an aristocrat, but the foregoing are sufficient for our purpose, as the three reasons given below may be taken as a *prima facie* case in favour of the Oxford authorship.

(1) Oxford died in 1604, and might therefore fairly be alluded to in 1609 as "our ever-living poet."

(2) For the same reason no protest by the author was possible.

(3) Sonnet No. CXI fits the case of a nobleman who occasionally acted on the public stage. We know, from Ben Jonson's play "Cynthia's Revels," that Amorphus —almost certainly a caricature of Oxford —occasionally did this.

Having established a *prima facie* case for the Earl of Oxford as the author of the Sonnets, let us examine the publication of them more closely, in the hope of obtaining further clues.

SHAKESPEARE AUTHORSHIP

The dedication reads as follows :

>   TO . THE . ONLIE . BEGETTER . OF
>   THESE . INSVING . SONNETS .
>   MR. . W.H. . ALL . HAPPINESSE .
>   AND . THAT . ETERNITIE .
>   PROMISED.
>   BY .
>   OVR . EVER-LIVING . POET .
>   WISHETH .
>   THE . WELL-WISHING .
>   ADVENTVRER . IN .
>   SETTING .
>   FORTH .
>   T.T.

The first sonnet, immediately following the dedication, opens thus :

From fairest creatures we desire increase,
That thereby beauty's rose might never die.

This opening sonnet is a recommendation to a young man to get married, and the dedication may be read as a wedding wish to " the onlie begetter," or procurer of the MS., to whom Thomas Thorpe wishes " all happinesse and that eternitie promised by our ever-living poet," which is the eternity obtainable by the " begetting " of posterity.

The individual to whom Thomas Thorpe wishes " all happinesse," etc., is " Mr. W.H." who is further described in the dedication as a " well-wishing " or hopeful " adventurer in setting forth " on his matrimonial adventure.

Who is this Mr. W.H. ?

It has been suggested with a considerable degree of plausibility that he was a certain William Hall, a member of the Stationers' Company, who in 1606 had procured for publication the MS. of " A Foure-fold Meditation," now known to have been written by Philip, Earl of Arundel, who died as a prisoner in the Tower in 1595.

As owner of the " copy," William Hall supplied a dedicatory epistle to the book over his initials, " W.H."

The wording of the Sonnet dedication, " Mr. W.H. ALL happinesse " is another indication that " W.H." stands for William Hall.

SHAKESPEARE AUTHORSHIP

If it be objected that a punning, frivolous dedication, such as this seems to be, is not in character with the ordinary Elizabethan dedication, it will be in order to quote from Christopher Marlowe's "First Book of Lucan," published by this same Thomas Thorpe in 1600. The dedication is signed by Thomas Thorpe as the publisher to his friend in the trade, Edward Blount, whom he addresses thus: "Blount, I purpose to be blunt with you."

If Thomas Thorpe could be facetious in one dedication to a fellow-publisher in 1600, why should he not adopt the same attitude to another brother stationer in 1609? We may take it therefore that a *prima facie* case in favour of Mr. William Hall as "Mr. W.H." has been established.

So far we have established two *prima facie* cases.

(1) That the Earl of Oxford was the author of the Sonnets.

(2) That the stationer, William Hall, was the "Mr. W.H." of the dedication.

SHAKESPEARE AUTHORSHIP

Can we prove these two cases by further circumstantial evidence ?

The following further facts now come into play :

(1) The Earl of Oxford was, at the time of his death in 1604, living at King's Place, Hackney.

(2) His widow, the Countess of Oxford, sold the house to Fulke Greville in 1609, and removed to Hedingham Castle in Essex.

It will be noticed that the year 1609, in which the house was sold, is the year in which the Sonnets were published. This at once supplies us with a fresh piece of evidence, for Lady Oxford's removal from King's Place provided just such an opportunity for the discovery of the manuscript of the poems as we might suppose would be taken advantage of by a publisher like William Hall, who three years previously had already procured for publication the manuscript of Arundel's " Foure-fold Meditation."

At this point it might be objected that

there is a gap in the evidence. No doubt it is quite true that if the opportunity had been presented to William Hall, he would have seized upon the chance either of publishing the Sonnets himself, as he did in the case of "A Fourefold Meditation," or of selling the rights of publication to another publisher; and we know that as a matter of fact it was this latter course that he actually pursued, for the Sonnets were published by Thomas Thorpe, another member of the Stationers' Company. But—and this is the first serious gap in the evidence—there is nothing so far to connect William Hall with King's Place, Hackney, the home of the Oxfords. It was at this point of the investigation that Colonel Ward decided to identify King's Place, and to see if the local records could provide any clue connecting William Hall with the locality. He has described his researches in "The Mystery of Mr. W.H.," pages 17-23, but they may be shortly epitomized as follows: he identified King's Place—now known as Brooke House—and confirmed from the local records the fact that the Countess of Oxford had

SHAKESPEARE AUTHORSHIP

sold it to Fulke Greville[1] in 1609. He was unable to find any reference to William Hall in the records preserved in the Central Library, Mare Street, Hackney, but he argued that as the Dedication to the Sonnets constituted a wedding wish to " Mr. W.H." it was possible—if he had been a native of Hackney—that his marriage might have taken place there. Accordingly, he went to the Parish Church, and examined the register of births, deaths, and marriages. The register of St. John-at-Hackney has been copied out and indexed by an enthusiastic parishioner, and therefore all that was necessary was to look out William Hall in the index. To this particular name there was only one reference, which read as follows :

> " William Hall and Margery Gryffyn were joyned in matrymonye on the 4th daye of August, 1608."

This piece of evidence may be said to have completely filled the gap, for it not only connected William Hall with Hackney, and

[1] Created Baron Brooke in 1621.

thus accounted for the possibility of his having obtained the manuscript of the Sonnets from King's Place, but, and this is surely the clinching piece of circumstantial evidence, he was married just nine months before " a book called Shakespeares Sonnettes " was entered on the Stationer's Register on the 20th May, 1609, and was therefore completely qualified as a " well-wishing adventurer setting forth " on his matrimonial adventure on the 4th August, 1608, to be the object of such a Dedication " to the onlie begetter " as Thomas Thorpe subsequently composed for his benefit, in recognition of his services in having procured for him a valuable manuscript of " our ever-living poet." I think it may be said that this discovery of William Hall's marriage at Hackney completely fills in the gap in the evidence, and proves beyond any reasonable doubt the truth of the two *prima facie* cases, which as we have already seen, Colonel Ward assumed as the basis of his researches, namely :

(1) That the Earl of Oxford was the author of the Sonnets.

(2) That the stationer, William Hall, was the "Mr. W.H." of the dedication.

He did not, however, cease his researches after the publication of "The Mystery of Mr. W.H." but continued to make further investigations. Up to the present time three more pieces of evidence have been found. The first of these pieces of evidence shows that a poem—"Faction that ever dwells"— originally printed in Nashe's surreptitious edition of Sidney's "Astrophel and Stella" in 1591, and attributed to Oxford at the time, was subsequently printed with slight alterations in a posthumous volume of Fulke Greville's poems in 1633. Now Fulke Greville occupied King's Place, Hackney, from 1609, when he purchased the house from Lady Oxford until his death in 1628. Two inferences follow from this fact:

(1) Oxford's poem, "Faction that ever dwells," was probably found at King Place after Fulke Greville's death and wrongly attributed to the last occupier of the house.

(2) If one of Oxford's poems, "Faction that ever dwells," was found at King's Place between 1628 and 1633, may not the same thing have happened in the case of the manuscript of Shakespeare's Sonnets in 1609, when Lady Oxford sold the house to Fulke Greville?

The second piece of evidence is contained in the following entry of a baptism in the Parish Register of St. Saviour's, Southwark:

1592, December 28, Margarett Gryffyn, daughter of Edward, a scryvener.

The name of the scrivener, Edward Gryffyn, occurs several times in Henslowe's Diary, and in the Henslowe Papers in connection with Henslowe, Alleyne, Daborne, Chettle, and other members of the underworld of Elizabethan writers and literary "begetters" to which Mr. W.H. belonged. This second piece of evidence adds to the probability that William Hall, who married Margery Gryffyn at Hackney on the 4th August, 1608, is the authentic "Mr. W.H." of "The Sonnets."

The third piece of evidence is provided by

SHAKESPEARE AUTHORSHIP

Sir Denys Bray's discovery of the true order of Shakespeare's Sonnets : [1]

We have already seen that the opening sonnet in the Quarto of 1609 is an invitation to a young man to get married. This marriage *motif* is carried on in the first seventeen sonnets of the series. This is what we should expect from the Dedication, which conveys a wedding wish to " Mr. W.H." Sir Denys Bray has, however, discovered that Sonnet No. 20 is really the first of the series.

In a recent article in " Poetry and The Play " (Vol. 13, No. 87. Winter, 1929-30), Colonel Ward has shown that this sonnet may be given the following heading :

> " The Poet receives intimation of the birth of his son."

Mr. Allen has adopted the same theory of the Sonnets in his recent book, " The Case for Edward de Vere as Shakespeare," and shows that the whole series is a dramatic representation of the poet's home life.

[1] " The Original Order of Shakespeare's Sonnets." Methuen & Co., 1925.

SHAKESPEARE AUTHORSHIP

As all the sonnets were written between about 1590 and 1604, they just fit the period of Oxford's second marriage, his son Henry having been born on the 24th February, 1593, and his own death having occurred in July, 1604. It will thus be seen that our inferences from Sir Denys Bray's discovery enable us to make the statements that here follow, confirming our two primary assumptions.

(1) The date of Oxford's second marriage and of the birth of his son fit in with the theory that he was the author.

(2) The alteration by Thomas Thorpe of the true order of the Sonnets, so as to make his opening sonnet fit the wedding wish of the Dedication, confirms our second assumption, namely, that the recently married William Hall was the " Mr. W.H." of the Dedication.

I will now complete my summing-up of the case with a recapitulation of the evidence for the Oxford authorship of the Sonnets.

(1) The entry in the Hackney Parish Register of the marriage of William Hall and Margery Gryffyn on the 4th August, 1608.

(2) The publication of an Oxford poem—" Faction that ever dwells "—in a posthumous volume of Fulke Greville's poems in 1633.

(3) The entry in the Parish Register of St. Saviour's, Southwark, of the birth of Margaret Gryffyn, daughter of Edward Gryffyn, a scrivener, on the 28th December, 1592.

(4) The discovery by Sir Denys Bray that Sonnet No. 20 in Thorpe's Quarto of 1609, is in reality the opening sonnet of the series.

Each one of these pieces of evidence points to the truth of one or other of our two *prima facie* assumptions, namely, that Oxford was the author of the Sonnets, and that William Hall was the " Mr. W.H." of the Dedication.

The story of the affair may be plausibly reconstructed thus: Oxford was living at King's Place, Hackney, from the date of his second marriage in 1591 to his death in 1604, his son Henry having been born in 1593.

All the Sonnets were written during this

period, and were left in manuscript at the time of his death.

When Lady Oxford vacated the house in 1609 the Sonnets came into the hands of William Hall, of Hackney, who had married the daughter of Henslowe's scrivener the year before. William Hall was a member of the Stationer's Company, but not being in a position at that time to publish them himself, he handed them over to his friend, Thomas Thorpe, who immediately published the volume with an amusing but ambiguous dedication to the "begetter" or procurer of the manuscript. In order to give point to the wedding wish of the Dedication he altered the true order of the Sonnets, and chose as the opening poem one that fitted in with the idea that the book was intended as a wedding gift to his fellow-publisher, William Hall, who was the actual "begetter" or procurer of the manuscript, and also a potential "begetter" of children to carry on his name.

We have now examined the case of the Sonnets thoroughly, and find that all the discoveries made during the last ten years, since Mr. Looney first propounded the theory that Oxford was Shakespeare, point in the direction of two main facts, namely, first the identification of Oxford as author of the Sonnets, and secondly the identification of William Hall as "Mr. W.H." of the Dedication.

I cannot do better than close by an adaptation of the remarks of the Lord Chief Justice in which he explained the meaning and scope of circumstantial evidence.

When we look at all the circumstances surrounding the publication of Shakespeare's Sonnets in 1609, we find such a series of undesigned, unexpected coincidences that—as reasonable persons—our judgment is compelled to one conclusion, and one conclusion only, and that is that their author, the "Shake-speare" of the title page, was none other than Edward de Vere, 17th Earl of Oxford.

SHAKESPEARE AUTHORSHIP

BIBLIOGRAPHY

"Prominent Points on the Life and Writings of Shakespeare."

By William Poel. Longmans, Green & Company, 1919.

A booklet of twelve pages containing notes on four Charts or Tables:

> Tables I and II, Facts and Traditions.
> Table III, Playhouses.
> Table IV, Plays.

An important foundation or point of departure for any discussion of the authorship question.

"'Shakespeare' Identified in Edward de Vere, the 17th Earl of Oxford."

By J. Thomas Looney. Cecil Palmer, 1920.

The following extract from the Introduction illustrates the scope and purpose of the book:

"At the beginning it was mainly the fascination of an interesting inquiry that held me, and the matter was pursued in the spirit of simple research. As the case has developed, however, it has tended increasingly to assume the form of a serious purpose, aiming at a long overdue act of justice and reparation to an unappreciated genius who, we believe, ought now to be put in possession of his rightful honours; and to whose memory should be accorded a gratitude proportionate to the benefits he has conferred upon mankind in general, and the lustre he has shed upon England in particular."

" The Poems of Edward de Vere."

With Notes by J. Thomas Looney. Cecil Palmer, 1921.

" The Mystery of Mr. W.H."

By Colonel B. R. Ward, C.M.G. Cecil Palmer, 1923.

Mainly an account of investigations carried out at Hackney during the summer of 1922.

" Shakespeare through Oxford Glasses."

By Captain H. H. Holland, C.B., Royal Navy. Cecil Palmer, 1923.

A study of topical allusions to the Earl of Oxford in the Shakespeare Plays.

SHAKESPEARE AUTHORSHIP

"The Original Order of Shakespeare's Sonnets."

By Sir Denys Bray, K.C.I.E. Methuen & Co., 1925.

An explanation of the rhyme-linked order in which the author undoubtedly intended the Sonnets to be read.

"A Hundreth Sundrie Flowres."

From the original edition of 1573, with Introduction and Notes by Captain B. M. Ward. Etchells and Macdonald, 1926. Captain Ward shows that the Earl of Oxford was the original editor, and author of seventeen of the poems, out of the total number of a hundred in the complete Anthology.

"The Shakespeare Mystery."

By George Connes. Abridged and translated into English by a member of the Shakespeare Fellowship. Cecil Palmer, 1927.

A statement of the various claims to Shakespeare authorship. The claims of the following individuals are examined:

SHAKESPEARE AUTHORSHIP

Francis Bacon,
Roger Manners, 5th Earl of Rutland,
William Stanley, 6th Earl of Derby,
Edward de Vere, 17th Earl of Oxford.

The author sums up in favour of the orthodox tradition.

"The Seventeenth Earl of Oxford." (1550-1604).

From Contemporary Documents. By Captain B. M. Ward. John Murray, 1928.

A full-length biography of the Earl of Oxford, based upon nearly five years' search among unpublished manuscript records of the time. A mine of information for all students of the Oxford claim.

"Shakespeare and Chapman as Topical Dramatists."

By Percy Allen. Cecil Palmer. 1929.

A study of topical allusions to contemporaries in the plays of Shakespeare and Chapman. The historic original of Hamlet is shown to be Edward de Vere.

SHAKESPEARE AUTHORSHIP

"The Case for Edward de Vere, 17th Earl of Oxford as 'William Shakespeare.'"

By Percy Allen. Cecil Palmer, 1930.

Mr. Allen's studies of Shakespeare and other Elizabethan writers resulting in the publication by him of two books, "Shakepeare, Jonson, and Wilkins as Borrowers" (1928), and "Shakespeare and Chapman as Topical Dramatists" (1929), have convinced him that Mr. Looney was right when, in "'Shakespeare' Identified," he argued that Edward de Vere, 17th Earl of Oxford, was the actual author of writings usually attributed to William Shakspere of Stratford. The following is a summary of the book:

Chapter
- I. Introductory.
- II. Oxford's Poems and Shakespeare.
- III. Shakespeare in the Lyrics of Lyly's Plays.
- IV. Oxford in "Venus and Adonis" and "Lucrece."
- V. Oxford in Chapman's Poems.

SHAKESPEARE AUTHORSHIP

   VI. Oxford in the Shakespearean Sonnets.

   VII. Oxford's Connection with Elizabethan Drama.

   VIII and IX. Oxford in some Shakepearean Comedies.

   X and XI. Oxford in some Shakepearean Tragedies.

   XII. Oxford in the Folio, and Summary.

THE SHAKESPEARE FELLOWSHIP.

President:
LIEUT.-COLONEL M. W. DOUGLAS, C.S.I., C.I.E.

Vice-Presidents:
Professor Abel Lefranc
Mr. J. Thomas Looney
Mr. L. J. Maxse.

OBJECTS OF THE FELLOWSHIP

The Fellowship was founded at Hackney on the 6th November, 1922, with the following objects:

1. To unite in one brotherhood all lovers of Shakespeare who are dissatisfied with the

prevailing Stratfordian orthodoxy, and who desire to see the principles of scientific historical criticism applied to the problem of Shakespearean authorship.

2. To encourage and to organize research among Parish Registers, wills, and other documents likely to throw light on the subject.

3. To form the nucleus of a Shakespeare reference library, and to collect lantern slides to be issued on loan for lecturing purposes.

MEMBERSHIP

Membership is open to all persons who sympathize with the objects of the Fellowship as detailed above.

SUBSCRIPTIONS

The annual subscription is 10s., due on the 1st November for the following year.

    COLONEL B. R. WARD, C.M.G.
     (*Honorary Secretary*)
    WYVENHOE,
    FARNHAM ROYAL,
    SLOUGH,
    BUCKS.

THE SEVENTEENTH EARL OF OXFORD
as the Author "WILLIAM SHAKESPEARE"

Mr. Percy Allen's studies of Shakespeare, and other Elizabethan writers, resulting in the publication by him of two books, "Shakespeare, Jonson and Wilkins as Borrowers" (1928), and "Shakespeare and Chapman as Topical Dramatists" (1929), have convinced him that Mr. J. T. Looney was right when, in "Shakespeare Identified," he argued that Edward de Vere, 17th Earl of Oxford, was the actual author of writings usually attributed to "William Shakespeare." Mr. Allen further pursues that line of research in his new book, which seems to establish an extremely powerful case.

THE CASE FOR EDWARD de VERE
(SEVENTEENTH EARL OF OXFORD)
AS SHAKESPEARE

By PERCY ALLEN

Crown 8vo.	7/6 net.	Cloth

CONTENTS.

CHAPTER	
I	Introductory.
II	Oxford's Poems and Shakespeare.
III	Shakespeare in the Lyrics of Lyly's Plays.
IV	Oxford in "Venus and Adonis" and "Lucrece."
V	Oxford in Chapman's Poems.
VI	Oxford in the Shakespearean Sonnets.
VII	Oxford's Connection with Elizabethan Drama.
VIII & IX	Oxford in Some Shakespearean Comedies.
X & XI	Oxford in Some Shakespearean Tragedies.
XII	Oxford in the Folio and Summary.

CECIL PALMER   **LONDON**

SHAKESPEARE, JONSON AND WILKINS AS BORROWERS

A Study in Elizabethan Dramatic Origins and Imitations.

By PERCY ALLEN

with an Introduction by Professor R. P. Cowl.

| Crown 8vo. | 7/6 net. | Cloth |

Times Literary Supplement.
> An intelligent and interesting book which should be of service to students of Elizabethan drama. We are over the frontier beyond literary scholarship.

Christian Science Monitor.
> This interesting book should become a standard work, and is certainly indispensable to students of Elizabethan drama. A masterly series of analytical and parallel studies.

Nation and Athenæum.
> His case, generally sound in itself, is clearly and scrupulously put .... Mr. Allen's reasoning and proofs are usually convincing.

SHAKESPEARE AND CHAPMAN AS TOPICAL DRAMATISTS

By PERCY ALLEN.

| Crown 8vo. | 7/6 net. | Cloth |

Mr. Percy Allen has followed up his recent book, " Shakespeare, Jonson, and Wilkins as Borrowers," with a second study.

SHAKESPEARE AND CHAPMAN AS TOPICAL DRAMATISTS. in which he endeavours to show the topical qualities and atmosphere of " Twelfth Night " and of " Hamlet," and to prove—in the case of " Twelfth Night," for the first time—the historic identities of their principal characters. Mr. Allen was given the clue to these investigations by a study of George Chapman's plays, " Bussy D'Ambois," " The Revenge of Bussy," and " Biron's Tragedy," in the course of which he saw that many of Shakespeare's plays, but particularly " Twelfth Night," " Macbeth," " Hamlet," and " Richard II," together with some of the historic originals of their characters also—are secretly commented upon, criticized, and imitated within Chapman's texts. Four chapters of Mr. Allen's book are devoted to an analysis of these intensely fascinating, and hitherto little investigated dramatic relations between Shakespeare and his rival poet; including what appears to be Chapman's identification of the Seventeenth Earl of Oxford, as the historic original of Hamlet.

CECIL PALMER   **LONDON**

SHAKESPEARE UNMASKED

THE SELF-NAMED WILLIAM SHAKE-SPEARE

THE PRINCE OF WALES

BORN LEGITIMATE AND UNACKNOWLEDGED:

SON OF H.M. QUEEN ELIZABETH and
THE EARL OF LEICESTER:

BAPTISED IN THE FALSE NAME OF
FRANCIS BACON:

PHILOSOPHER, DRAMATIST, POET and ARCH-MARTYR

THEREAFTER NAMED

VISCOUNT ST. ALBANS

BY
ALFRED MUDIE

Demy 8vo.	5/- net	Boards

THE SHAKESPEARE MYSTERY

By Pro. Georges Connes
(University of Dijon)
(Abridged and translated into English by a Member of the Shakespeare Fellowship)

Crown 8vo.	7/6 net.	Cloth

"To summarise in less than 300 pages the innumerable and not infrequently tedious and complicated arguments in favour of this or that claimant for Shakespeare honours, and to give due weight to each one, was a task calling for peculiar qualities; fortunate in possessing them, M. Connes has written a book of value to students of Shakespeare and of real interest even to those who care not at all whether Shakespeare or another wrote the plays."—*Times Literary Supplement*.

CECIL PALMER	LONDON

THE SHAKESPEARE CONTROVERSY

THE STRATFORD BUST AND THE DROESHOUT ENGRAVING.

By Sir George Greenwood.

Crown 8vo.   2/6 net.   Cloth

The book presents a clear sifting of evidence to a logical conclusion, as to the authenticity or otherwise of the Stratford Bust and the Droeshout Engraving as true portraits of the Great Poet.

"SHAKESPEARE" IDENTIFIED IN EDWARD DE VERE, the Seventeenth Earl of Oxford. By J. Thomas Looney. Demy 8vo. 21/- net.

THE POEMS OF EDWARD DE VERE, Seventeenth Earl of Oxford. With Biographical Notice, Introduction to the Poems and Notes by J. Thomas Looney. Demy 8vo. 7/- net.

BEN JONSON AND SHAKESPEARE. By Sir George Greenwood. Crown 8vo. 3/6 net.

SHAKESPEARE'S LAW. By Sir George Greenwood. Crown 8vo. 2/6 net.

LEE, SHAKESPEARE, AND A TERTIUM QUID. By Sir George Greenwood. Crown 8vo. 5/- net.

SHAKESPEARE'S SIGNATURE AND "SIR THOMAS MORE." By Sir George Greenwood. Crown 8vo. 5/- net.

SHAKESPEARE THROUGH OXFORD GLASSES. By Rear-Admiral H. H. Holland, C.B. Crown 8vo. 7/6 net.

BACONIAN ESSAYS. By Edward W. Smithson. Edited, with an Introduction and two Essays, by Sir George Greenwood. Demy 8vo. 12/6 net.

THE MYSTERY OF "MR. W. H." By Colonel B. R. Ward, C.M.G. With 12 illustrations. F'cap 4to. 10/6 net.

THE COUNTESSE OF PEMBROKE'S ARCADIA : Examined and Discussed by the late Edward George Harman, C.B. With a chapter on Thomas Lodge. Demy 8vo. 12/6 net.

THE IMPERSONALITY OF SHAKESPEARE. By the late Edward George Harman, C.B. Demy 8vo. 12/6 net.

CECIL PALMER   LONDON

"SHAKE-SPEARES" SONNETS UNMASKED

Crown 8vo   By BERTRAM G. THEOBALD, B.A.   5/- *net.*   Cloth

"Mr. Theobald's Book . . . is intensely interesting."—*Manchester City News.*
"A book that all may read who would go into the controversy of the authorship of Shakespeare Plays."—*Publishers' Circular.*
"A striking theory for lovers of ingenuity."—*T.P.'s and Cassell's Weekly.*

---

1   **MUMMY'S BEDTIME STORY BOOK**
By "MARION." Illustrated on every page in four colours by JESSIE M. KING. A volume of delightful stories for children told with whimsical charm and a winning simplicity. Beautifully illustrated by a famous artist. Demy 4to. 5s. net. Illustrated Boards.

2   **LITTLE FAIRY DAYDREAMS**
By UNA ROSAMOND (MRS. A. S. M. HUTCHINSON). Illustrated with full-page drawings by DOUGLAS L. DICK. A little girl's adventures in Fairyland with the Dream Fairies, where she meets Mother Goose, Little Jack Horner, The Three Blind Mice, and many other familiar friends. An ideal gift book by the wife of the famous author of "If Winter Comes." Cr. 4to. 5s. net. Cloth Boards.

3   **WONDERFUL DAYS**
By AUSTIN LATHAM. Illustrated throughout by MURIEL DAWSON. Those who loved A. A. MILNE's "When We Were Very Young" will adore this book. Exquisite poems of Childhood and perfectly illustrated by a fine artist. Demy 8vo. 5s. net. Cloth.

4   **A CHILD'S ROBERT LOUIS STEVENSON**
By PATRICK BRAYBROOKE. Arranged with Notes, Life, and Glossary. Cr. 8vo. Cloth. Frontispiece portrait. 7/6 net.

"Mr. Braybrooke . . . has produced an anthology which may well lead many of the younger generation to a more extended enjoyment and understanding of R.L.S."—*Dublin Evening Mail.*
"Written in such a gleeful fashion, with such thrills . . . that one gasps in amazement . . . The work is most fascinating."—*Birkenhead News.*

5   **THE ROSY FINGERS**
By COLONEL ARTHUR LYNCH. Contains graphic personal touches of Kruger, Botha, Lloyd George, Ramsay MacDonald, Trotsky, G. B. Shaw, Lord Balfour and Lord Birkenhead. Cr. 8vo. 7/6 net. Cloth.

6 ROMANTIC CEYLON: in History, Legend and Story
By R. H. BASSETT. This is not a "Travel" book; it is Ceylon from the inside. Demy 8vo. Cloth. 7/6 net. Illustrated.

7   **LOVE SMUGGLERS AND NAVAL HEROES**
Being Historical Notes of the 18th Century.
By LILIAN BOYS BEHRENS. Author of "Under Thirty-Seven Kings." This book contains legends and amusing anecdotes with genuine 18th-century history centred round some Naval Heroes, principally of the families of Lamb. Cr. 8vo. 7/6 net. Illustrated.

CECIL PALMER   **LONDON**